Sept 2016

to Aviv

Mom & Dad all your

hopes & dreams come

true!

Shadow

The Curious Morgan Horse

By Ellen F. Feld

Illustrated by Jeanne Mellin

Willow Bend Publishing ● Goshen, Massachusetts

To Rusty—
a very special Morgan Horse.

E.F.F.

To Nancy—
for carrying on the Morgan Horse tradition so well.

J.M.

Copyright © 2012 by Ellen F. Feld

Published by Willow Bend Publishing, P.O. Box 304, Goshen, MA 01032
www.willowbendpublishing.com

Illustrations by Jeanne Mellin

Design and art direction by Linda Mahoney

Library of Congress Control Number: 2012935619

ISBN: 978-0-9831138-3-6

Printed in Korea

10 9 8 7 6 5 4 3 2

One beautiful spring morning, on the hill behind the big, red barn, a baby horse was born. Her name was Shadow, and like her mother Frosty, she was a Morgan Horse. She had tiny little hooves, soft gray hair covering her body, and long, curly whiskers at the tip of her nose. Her mane and tail were black, and she had the brightest blue eyes that her mother had ever seen.

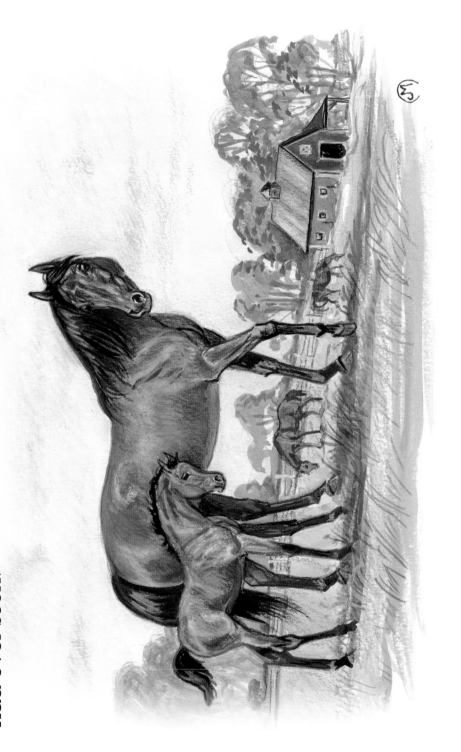

5

Shadow loved to run and play in the field where she and her mother lived. She would jump towards the sky, kick her back feet up high, and chase the butterflies who flew into her pasture. Shadow would run, and run, and run until she came within a few inches of the wooden fence that surrounded her home. Then she would stop and stare at the mysterious woods beyond the fence. How she wanted to travel into the woods to see what lived among its tall trees!

One day, the rooster who lived in the barn wandered into Shadow's field and told the young horse about his amazing adventures in the woods beyond the fence.

"You really went into the woods?" asked Shadow in disbelief.

"Yes, many times," answered the rooster as he puffed out his chest. "In fact, the last time I traveled into the woods was yesterday. I was gone for several hours and met lots of wild animals."

"Did you see a bear?" asked the curious horse.

"Yes!" exclaimed the rooster.

"Did he scare you?" asked Shadow.

"He roared at me, but I wasn't afraid. I cock-a-doodle-dooed and he ran away," bragged the rooster as he puffed his chest out even further. "Then I met a deer who showed me a magical pond. The water sparkled and the deer told me that anybody who drank from the pond could fly!"

"Wow!" exclaimed Shadow. "Did you drink the water?"

"No," said the rooster. "It was getting dark and I had to go home." The rooster scratched the ground with his bright yellow feet and then turned and walked away.

As Shadow watched the rooster return to the barn, she decided that she wanted to go into the woods to find the amazing pond.

Later that day, when Shadow told her mother Frosty about the magical pond, her mother just smiled and scratched Shadow's neck with her teeth. Frosty knew that the rooster had never gone beyond the fence. The rooster was really a silly bird who was afraid to leave the safety of the barnyard. Every day he made up stories of his wild adventures because he thought it made the other animals like him.

When Frosty told Shadow about the rooster's stories, the young horse refused to believe her mother. "Why would he make up stories?" asked Shadow. "I know there's a magical pond. I just know it!" she exclaimed as she ran off to chase a butterfly.

The next day, the sky was filled with storm clouds. The wind began to blow and soon the rain was falling. There was lightning and thunder crashing all around the horses.

Shadow clung to her mother's side, waiting for the storm to pass. Suddenly, Shadow heard such a loud crashing sound that she jumped. "Mommy," she said softly, "I'm scared."

"It's okay," replied Frosty. "It was only a tree falling to the ground. The storm will be over soon." But Shadow, still very frightened, closed her eyes and pushed closer to her mother.

Finally, the rain stopped and the roar of thunder drifted far away. The storm was over. Shadow opened her eyes and looked at her mother. Frosty smiled, nuzzled her baby, and began to eat grass.

Shadow was so happy that the storm had ended. She ran, and ran, and ran all around her pasture. As she approached the far corner of her home, she saw something that she needed to explore. The tree they had heard falling during the storm had crashed into the fence.

The curious baby slowed to a walk and then carefully approached the tree. A small section of the fence lay flat on the ground under the tree. She sniffed the tree and touched it with her long nose whiskers. Shadow decided it was safe and stepped over the lowest branch. In an instant she was on the other side of her pasture. Looking back, she saw her mother peacefully grazing on the lush, green grass.

"Now I can explore!" exclaimed the young Morgan Horse as she ran away towards the woods.

Shadow moved quickly into the woods. She hoped to meet lots of interesting wild animals. Could she find the magical pond? Would drinking its water really make her fly? The young horse thought about the pond as she ran and kicked up her hooves.

Shadow followed a wide path that was covered with a blanket of pine needles that tickled her feet. She giggled and laughed as the pine needles crunched. What fun it was to play in the woods!

Suddenly, Shadow saw the most amazing yellow flower. It was a very tall flower with enormous yellow petals and a bright pink middle. The curious horse stopped to get a better look. She could smell the lovely fragrance that drifted from the flower.

Shadow walked up to the flower and put her nose right up against the bright, yellow petals. She sniffed its perfume.

"Wow! What a nice smell!" she exclaimed. "It smells so —hey!" she suddenly squealed, "that hurts!"

Shadow jumped away from the flower, her nose stinging with pain. "What was that?" she asked.

Then she saw a small, fuzzy creature with a big black and yellow belly crawl out from his hiding place underneath the petals.

"You were sticking your nose into my house," bellowed the bumblebee, "and I didn't like that!"

"You stung me?" asked Shadow, unable to believe that such a small animal could make her nose hurt so much.

"Yes!" replied the bumblebee. "And I'll do it again if you come any closer," he threatened as he stretched out his wings, getting ready to fly.

"Fine," grumbled Shadow. "I'll leave," she said as she walked away. Heading deeper into the woods, Shadow tried to forget about the grouchy bumblebee.

Walking along, Shadow heard the sound of a stick breaking. Looking over to the side, she saw a small deer.

"Hi!" shouted Shadow.

"Oh my gosh," replied the baby deer, "I didn't see you there. What are you?"

"I'm a horse," answered Shadow. "And you're a deer, right?"

"Yes, I am a deer."

"Do you live in the woods?" asked Shadow.

"Yes, with my mother."

"That must be so neat," said Shadow.

Just then, the young deer's mother came out from behind a large bush. "Pepper, who are you talking to?"

"A new friend, Mom," replied the baby deer.

"Don't you remember that you're not allowed to talk to strangers?" scolded the deer's mother. "Come on now, it is time to go to the pond."

"The pond? The magic pond? Can I come?" asked Shadow. But the two deer had jumped off the path and behind the trees so quickly that Shadow didn't have a chance to go along. "I guess I'll have to try and follow their trail," she told herself.

Shadow slowly made her way through the thick underbrush. There were fallen branches, rocks, and overgrown bushes everywhere. It made traveling very hard. After what seemed like a long time, Shadow stumbled back onto a path. Was it the one she was on before? She didn't know.

Was she lost?

Seeing a small black animal with a big white stripe down its back, Shadow asked the creature, "Do you know how to get to the magic pond?"

"Magic pond? Magic pond? I've never heard of a magic pond," grumbled the little animal. "And I don't like being bothered!" he complained as he lifted his tail and squirted an obnoxious smelling liquid towards Shadow.

"Ew! Ew! Ew!" shouted the surprised horse. "That smells terrible," she moaned as she raised her head towards the sky and curled her lip. "Gross! Gross! Gross!"

"Don't you know you should never bother a skunk?" asked the fluffy skunk as he waddled off.

"Oh, this isn't fun at all!" mumbled Shadow as the horrible smell filled the air.

Shadow decided to run down the path to get away from the awful fumes. She ran, and ran, and ran, but this time she wasn't chasing a butterfly and she wasn't having fun. She was trying to get away from the awful smell.

Finally the skunk smell disappeared and Shadow slowed to a walk. Looking far in the distance, she saw a lot of tall, green grass.

"A field?" she asked herself. "Out here in the woods? I better go explore!" and off she went again.

The curious horse quickly came to a little field, with grass growing everywhere. But the most exciting thing was that there was a small pond in the center of the field. At the far corner of the pond were the two deer who she had met earlier during her adventure.

"I found the magic pond!" she shouted.

The sudden noise frightened the deer who had not seen the horse approach. Their heads shot up from the water, and both the mother and baby deer looked at Shadow. Then, in an instant, they turned and dashed away.

"Wait! Why are you leaving?" asked Shadow. But it was too late. The deer were gone. "I wonder why they didn't fly away?" Shadow asked herself. "After all, they did drink from the magic pond."

Deciding that it was time to try drinking the water, Shadow ran into the water, up to her belly. She lowered her head and took a big gulp of water. She paused for a moment, then raised her head.

"Hmmm....," she mumbled. "I don't feel any different. Maybe I need to drink more water." Shadow put her whole nose into the pond and drank, and drank, and drank until her tummy hurt.

"Oh," she moaned. "I have a terrible stomach ache." But did she feel any different? Could she fly now? "I have so much water in my belly that I don't think I could ever fly."

"Fly? Fly? What makes you think you can fly?"

"Who said that?" Shadow asked as she turned in the direction of the voice.

"I did," said a short, pudgy, brown, white, and black dog who was standing at the edge of the pond, right in front of Shadow. The dog's ears were so long that

they almost touched the ground, and she had the saddest looking eyes. She also had stubby little legs and a long nose that clung to the ground. "My name is Willow."

"Hi, Willow. My name is Shadow."

"Nice to meet you Shadow. Now, as I already asked, what makes you think you can fly?"

"I just drank water from the magic pond. The rooster at our farm told me if I drank from this pond I could fly."

"Well," explained the dog, "the rooster must have been making up a story. This isn't a magic pond. This is simply a pond where the animals of the forest get their water."

"You mean I can't fly?" asked a disappointed Shadow.

"Go ahead and try," suggested the dog.

Shadow thought about how she should try flying. Should she run fast? Splash in the water? Maybe if she got her whole body wet with the magic water, it would work better.

She decided to splash around in the pond and started kicking at the water with all four legs. As she moved around, however, her feet sunk deeper and deeper into the mud on the bottom of the pond.

Suddenly, Shadow felt herself sinking. "Help! Willow! Help! What do I do?"

"Shadow! Stop splashing!" yelled Willow. "You are sinking because of all your splashing."

Shadow did as Willow suggested. But she could still feel the mud sucking her feet down further.

"Now what?" she asked in a panic.

"Pick up one foot at a time and walk toward me," instructed the dog.

Shadow slowly picked up one of her front feet. She could feel the mud trying to hold onto her foot, but soon it let go and her foot was free. She stepped forward and then did the same with her other front foot. It was working!

Getting out of the water seemed to take forever and Shadow was so happy once she had all four feet up on shore. She smiled at the dog and thanked her for all the help.

"Now, I think I better go home," announced the horse.

"What's wrong?" asked Willow when she noticed that Shadow wasn't moving.

"I don't know which way to go. I think I'm lost," answered the frightened horse.

"I'll get you home," said Willow. "I'm a basset hound and I've got a great nose. I can find your scent and follow the trail to your home."

"Would you really?" asked the nervous horse.

"Sure, I'd be happy to help you," said Willow as she wagged her tail. Putting her nose to the ground, Willow began to walk around. She went this way, then that, all over the field.

Finally, she let out a loud bark. "I have it! I found your scent! Now we can follow it all the way to your home."

Shadow eagerly followed the basset hound. They went back into the woods and soon came to a spot that smelled terrible.

"My goodness," groaned Willow. "What is that awful smell? Did you find a skunk?"

Shadow nodded her head and Willow laughed.

Soon, Willow wandered off the path towards the place where Shadow had met the deer. Then they were back on another path, passing the big, yellow flower where the bumblebee lived. Finally, they came out into the bright sunshine, along the edge of Shadow's pasture.

"I'm home! I'm home!" she said excitedly as she raced to the fallen tree and carefully crossed over the broken fence into her pasture. Willow followed her new friend.

At the other end of the field, Shadow could see her mother. Frosty was running along the fence, whinnying and calling out for her daughter. "Mom! I'm down here!"

Hearing her daughter's voice, Frosty turned and then ran, full-speed, toward the young horse. "Shadow! Where have you been? I've been so worried about you."

Shadow told her mother all about her trip and introduced Frosty to Willow. "She helped me get home, Mom. I don't know what I would have done without Willow."

Frosty gently scratched Shadow's back with her teeth and told the baby how much she loved her. Then she made the youngster promise never, ever to go exploring without her mother.

"I promise Mom," smiled Shadow.

"And Willow," said Shadow as she looked at the basset hound, "thank you so much for showing me how to get home!"

Willow smiled and wagged her tail.

The next day, the fence had been fixed and Shadow no longer wanted to wander off by herself. Instead, she ran, and ran, and ran, chasing butterflies, with Willow, her new friend, by her side.